ELECTRICITY IN ACTION

WATT'S UP?
ELECTRICITY AT WORK

by Jenny Mason

CAPSTONE PRESS
a capstone imprint

Published by Capstone Press, an imprint of Capstone
1710 Roe Crest Drive, North Mankato, Minnesota 56003
capstonepub.com

Copyright © 2026 by Capstone. All rights reserved. No part of this publication may be reproduced in whole or in part, or stored in a retrieval system, or transmitted in any form or by any means, electronic, mechanical, photocopying, recording, or otherwise, without written permission of the publisher.

Library of Congress Cataloging-in-Publication Data is available on the Library of Congress website.

ISBN: 9798875222467 (hardcover)
ISBN: 9798875222412 (paperback)
ISBN: 9798875222429 (ebook PDF)

Summary: Readers discover how electricity powers homes, gadgets, and machines, and explore the ways electricity is generated and used in everyday life.

Editorial Credits
Editor: Ericka Smith; Designer: Sarah Bennett; Media Researcher: Jo Miller; Production Specialist: Tori Abraham

Image Credits
Getty Images: Martin Puddy, cover, Chalffy, 22, iStock/Bet_Noire, 18, iStock/Herculeru, 10, iStock/jinjo0222988, 21, iStock/VladimirFLoyd, 15 (bottom), iStock/wasabi Takada, 11, Keystone, 15 (top), Luis Alvarez, 24, Martin Puddy, cover, Photos.com, 12 (bottom right), Steve Smith, 23, valentinrussanov, 17; Shutterstock: AsiaTravel, 29, Bits And Splits, 20 (spool), cyo bo, 26, DestinaDesign, 12 (top right), EWY Media, 16, hramovnick, 8, hrui, 9, Kung37, 20 (battery), Lekdood, 20 (disc magnets), NicoElNino, 27, Papia Majumder, 7, Vectomart, 4

Design Elements
Shutterstock: galihprihatama, Iurii Motov

Any additional websites and resources referenced in this book are not maintained, authorized, or sponsored by Capstone. All product and company names are trademarks™ or registered® trademarks of their respective holders.

Table of Contents

INTRODUCTION
HIDDEN POWERS..........................4

CHAPTER 1
POWER SUPPLY 6

CHAPTER 2
FROM BRIGHT IDEAS TO SENDING SIGNALS.... 14

CHAPTER 3
MARCH OF THE MACHINES................18

CHAPTER 4
POWER TRIPS 26

GLOSSARY......................30
READ MORE 31
INTERNET SITES 31
INDEX 32
ABOUT THE AUTHOR.............32

Words in **bold** are in the glossary.

INTRODUCTION
HIDDEN POWERS

Zip. Blip. The power's out! Suddenly, you have no lights, TV, or Internet. And there's no hot water for a shower! Traffic lights wink off. Subway trains stop. Businesses shut down.

Your home, restaurants, schools, hospitals, and transportation rely on electricity. Electricity is a natural energy people first harnessed about 200 years ago. Since then, people have come up with clever ways to transport and use electricity to power our world.

Subatomic Charges

Protons have a positive charge. Electrons have a negative charge. And neutrons are neutral. Like charges repel each other, while opposite charges attract each other.

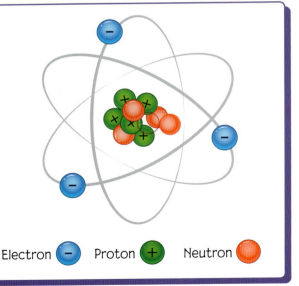

WHAT'S THE BUZZ ON ELECTRICITY?

What is electricity?

Electricity is a natural force. It can be used to make light and heat or to make machines work.

Where does electricity come from?

Everything in the universe is made of super-tiny building blocks called **atoms**. Each atom has **protons**, **neutrons**, and **electrons**. Sometimes, electrons can move from one atom to the next. That movement creates electricity.

What's the difference between a conductor and insulator?

Electricity moves through **conductors**. Conductors are materials that help electrons flow easily. Water and certain metals are conductors. **Insulators** slow or stop the flow of electrons. Wood, plastic, and rubber are insulators.

How is electricity measured?

Amps tell you how quickly the electrons are moving. Volts tell you how much pressure there is on the electrons. The energy of electricity can be put to work. The difficulty of the work is measured in watts.

Watts = Amps x Volts

CHAPTER 1
POWER SUPPLY

When you flip a light switch, a bulb shines instantly. Electricity is the energy feeding that light. The electricity that helps power your home comes from a power station. Power stations "wake up" electricity and get it moving. They use special machines called **turbine generators** to get electrical energy moving.

Generating Electricity

Turbine generators rely on a simple idea—changing the energy of movement into electrical energy. But it requires a lot of steps and parts.

Boiler: Fuels are burned to boil water. Smoke from the burnt fuel is released through a smokestack.

Pipes: Steam from the boiling water moves through pipes at high speeds.

Turbine: The steam whooshes through turbines, which are made of many fan blades. The blades whirl around. The steam condenses to warm water and falls into a condenser.

Rotor: The blades are attached to a long rod or rotor. The rotor spins too.

Generator: Magnets attached to the rotor whirl round and round. This motion creates a magnetic field of energy.

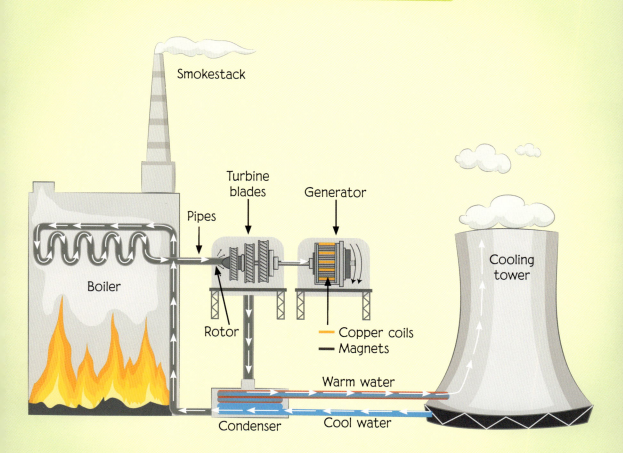

Coils: Wreaths of coiled copper wire surround the spinning magnets. The electrons in the copper are excited by the magnetic field. They flow through the wire. This flow is an electrical current that will pass along huge wires to towns and cities.

Cooling Tower: After moving the turbine blades, the steam moves to a cooling tower. When it cools, it changes back to water. That water is recycled back to the boiler.

A generator in a power station lights up with power.

Steam escapes from cooling towers at a power plant.

FACT

Besides burning fuels, power stations can also use fast-flowing water to spin turbines, or they can capture energy from the sun or wind.

Building a Charge

Power station generators build up a big electric charge. Imagine shaking up a bottle of soda. The more you shake, the more bubbles form. The pressure in the bottle rises. The pressure of electricity is known as **voltage**. The bigger the pressure, the higher the voltage. To release the pressure, the electric charge is shot out on large, long wires.

A Couple of Stops

The high-voltage power moves to a substation. These are neighborhood power facilities. They turn down the voltage of the electrical current. Then, they send that power to homes, schools, and offices using more wires, or transmission lines.

An electrical transformer substation

Electrical energy makes one last stop on the journey to your home. It passes through a step-down transformer. These devices reduce the voltage yet again before it enters a building.

A transformer on a power line

FACT

Electricity traveling along power lines can reach up to 765,000 volts. Transformers trim it down to 110 volts for people to safely use.

Battery Power

Batteries are another way we make and store electricity. Cell phones, laptops, and clocks all use batteries. Chemicals inside the battery separate electrons and protons. Electrons are shoved towards the negative **terminal**. The protons bunch up at the positive terminal. The like particles push away from each other. But the electrons and protons never stop trying to reconnect. This constant pushing and pulling creates electric energy. It is trapped until a wire connects the terminals and forms a **circuit**. The electrons escape and flow back to the protons. The circuit can power other devices.

FACT

Alessandro Volta made the first battery in 1800. He stacked, or piled, metal discs and paper sheets soaked in salt water. Volts, or the measure of electric energy's pressure, is named in his honor.

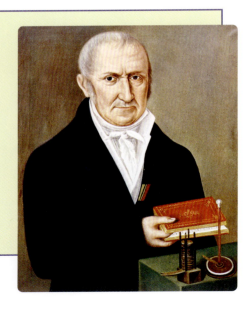

Make a Battery

Make your own "voltaic pile" battery using coins and lemon juice. You'll need an adult's help for this activity.

Heads Up! Metal tweezers conduct electricity. A rubber handle protects you from getting zapped.

Supplies:
- scissors
- a paper towel
- tin foil
- 10-15 clean pennies
- 10-15 clean nickels
- lemon juice
- rubber-handled tweezers
- an LED bulb

Steps:

1. Cut small circles out of a sheet of paper towel. The circles should be slightly smaller than a penny.

2. Cut a strip of foil. Place a penny on it.

3. Dip a paper-towel circle in the lemon juice. (Use the tweezers if needed.) Tap away any excess liquid that drips from the circle.

4. Place the wet circle on top of the penny. Place a nickel on top of the circle. You have made one battery cell!

5. Make another battery cell by stacking a penny on the nickel. Add another piece of soaked paper and another nickel.

6. Touch the longer (positive) LED leg to the foil. Touch the shorter (negative) leg to the top of the coin stack. Use tweezers to hold one leg. (Bend the LED legs if needed.) If the light does not flicker on, add more cells. More cells build up more voltage.

7. Try making a battery with five cells. If that doesn't work, keep adding cells. How many cells did you need to power the LED light?

CHAPTER 2
FROM BRIGHT IDEAS TO SENDING SIGNALS

In the 1800s, scientists experimented with uses for electric currents. Their efforts often produced sparks, or bursts of light. Sparks occur when charged electrons jump through the air. Inventors created special lamps that produced constant sparks. These arc lights lit up city streets and farms.

People wanted electric light in their homes. But arc lights were too bright, and wild sparks sometimes started fires. So inventors looked for a better solution.

Glow with the Flow

To make better lights, scientists experimented with **semiconductors**. These materials slow down an electric current. The slower electric energy heats the semiconductor and causes it to glow.

The earliest light bulbs contained hot, glowing wires called filaments. The glass bulb protected people from a serious burn.

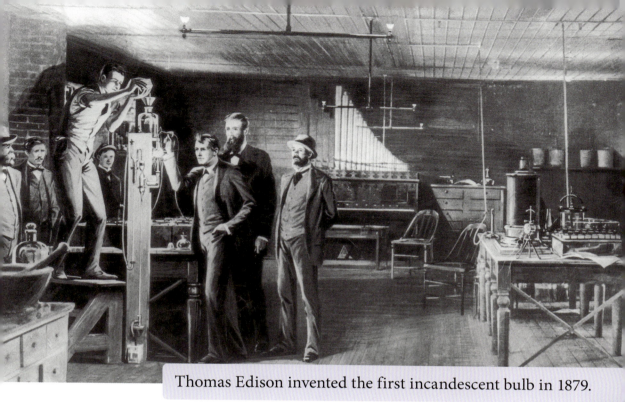

Thomas Edison invented the first incandescent bulb in 1879.

Over time, newer lights passed an electric current across gasses in the bulb. Streetlights use these bulbs. Today's LEDs make electrons hopscotch across many atoms. This hopping creates a bright light.

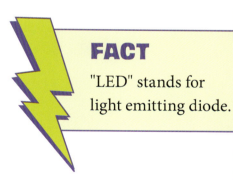

FACT
"LED" stands for light emitting diode.

Evolution of lighting

15

Electric Communication

Experiments with electricity also led to new ways of communicating. Early devices, like the **telegraph**, sent electrical pulses through a wire. The pulses represented letters that spelled out words.

Alexander Graham Bell's harmonic telegraph receiver

Later, the telephone turned a person's voice into an electrical signal that could travel long distances over wires. Radio broadcasts beamed spoken words and music through the air.

Now, the Internet we rely on is actually information turned into electric signals. Can you imagine life without electric light or the Internet?

A teen practices guitar with an online tutorial.

CHAPTER 3

MARCH OF THE MACHINES

Bing! Pop! Your toast is ready. Electricity heats the wires that toast the bread. Those wires are like lighting filaments.

All of your household appliances run on electricity.

Other gadgets turn electric energy into motion. The fan in a hair dryer spins. Washing machines and dryers spin or tumble clothes. Electricity powers the pumps that shoot water from the shower or sink faucets. Blenders, microwaves, vacuum cleaners, heaters, air conditioners—these machines all run on electrified motors.

The Power of Magnets

Electric motors harness two forces of the universe. One is electricity. The other is magnetism. Electric currents create magnetic energy. Magnets have opposite charges, or poles. Like poles repel each other. Opposites attract. Motors pass a current through ordinary metal plates which turns them into pushing-pulling magnets. The plates are arranged in a ring to make the magnetic energy spin. That spin spreads to gears that get work done. Blender blades whirl. The dryer drum tumbles clothes.

Make an Electromagnetic Motor

Electricity. Magnetism. Movement. All three elements combine inside electric motors. Watch them interact when you make your own electromagnetic motor. But first, ask an adult to help you with this activity.

Supplies:
- 1 spool of 22-gauge or less copper wire at least 5 feet (1.5 meters) long
- 1 AA battery
- 6 disc or coin magnets
- 1 pair of mechanic's gloves

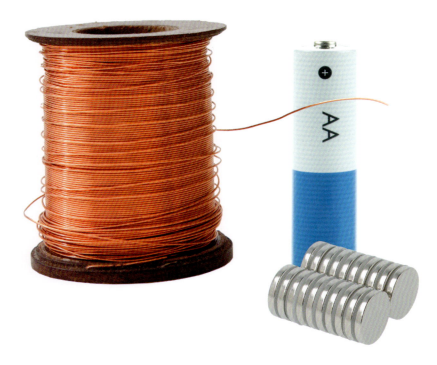

Steps:

1. Shape the copper wire into a long, closely wrapped coil. Make sure the AA battery can fit comfortably inside the coil.

2. Attach three coin magnets to both ends of the AA battery.

3. Slide the AA battery-magnet into the coil. Watch as it whizzes through the copper "tunnel."

4. Wearing the gloves, hold both ends of the coil tunnel together to create an endless loop for the battery to race around! (Note: the gloves protect you from heat building up in the wire, not shocks.)

5. Why does it work? The magnets release the electric energy in the battery. The electric current boosts their magnetism. The copper wire conducts the electricity which also briefly magnetizes it. It magnetically repels one magnet stack and pulls the other.

Electrified Factories

Electric machines in factories freed workers from tough, repetitive jobs. Machines worked faster. They also did not need a break to rest. Clothes. Candy. Railroad tracks. Automobiles. Factories churned out all these things and more. Making products faster also made them cheaper to buy.

Automobile factories use many electrical machines.

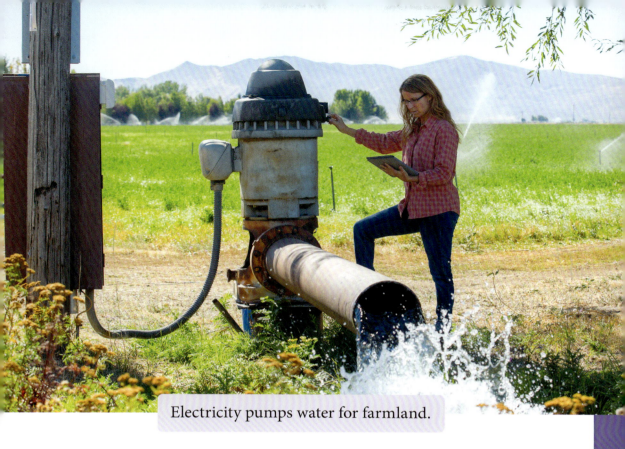

Electricity pumps water for farmland.

Old Zap-Donald Had a Farm

Not long ago, farms were small. People plowed fields and watered and harvested crops by hand. They also used animals like horses, oxen, or mules. Motorized machines changed farming. Tractors plowed bigger areas more quickly. Electric pumps delivered water.

Today, electricity also air conditions indoor rooms for pigs, chickens, and other livestock. It heats fruits or veggies when the weather turns chilly. Electricity helps farms produce more food than ever before.

The Power to Save Lives

Does thinking of a hospital make you imagine lots of beeping, clicking, and pulsing devices? Today, doctors and nurses rely on electricity to save lives. Electric sensors track blood flow, heart rate, and brain activity. Other machines take over when an organ cannot do its job. For example, a respirator can breathe for the lungs. Special waves of electric energy "see" directly inside a person's body. X-rays take pictures of your bones.

Magical Electrical Medicine

About 2,000 years ago, early civilizations treated some medical conditions using electric fish or eels. Patients endured painful electric shocks from these animals. Modern electric medicine has come a long way. Specialists use gentle electric pulses on the brain to reverse blindness. They can sometimes bring movement back to paralyzed muscles. Tiny electric devices can nest inside the body. Their pulses help different organs function. For example, a cochlear implant functions like parts of the inner ear. It helps deaf people hear.

Electric Medical Marvels

1885 X-rays capture images of bones, and heart monitors use electricity to detect a heartbeat.

1927 Respirators help the lungs breathe.

1933 Machines called defibrillators jolt a heart with electricity to make it beat again.

1945 A machine that filters toxins from the blood can be used when the kidneys stop working.

1959 Ultrasounds use special electric waves to view babies developing inside women's bodies.

1970s MRI and CT machines are used to see into bodies.

1987 Electric beams called lasers make cuts in eye surgeries.

1994 Smart pills—capsules with medicine, electric sensors, or even cameras—help diagnose, treat, and track illnesses.

2000 Robots assisted by medical professionals perform surgeries on people.

2014 3D printers use human tissues to create new skin, livers, and even teeth.

2022 Doctors use artificial intelligence (AI) to diagnose illnesses. Electricity powers these ultra-fast computer programs.

FACT

"CT" stands for computerized tomography.
"MRI" stands for magnetic resonance imaging.

CHAPTER 4
POWER TRIPS

Swooooosh! A magnetic levitation (maglev) train darts across the glittering city of Shanghai, China. These trains are the world's fastest because they float using electromagnetic power. They can reach speeds up to 270 miles (435 kilometers) per hour.

A maglev train zooms through Shanghai, China.

FACT

A maglev train could travel from New York City to Los Angeles in just seven hours! But the world's six maglev trains are only in Asia.

With electricity, people travel and see farther than ever before in history. Airplanes and sea vessels use electrical instruments to navigate. Batteries power the thousands of satellites swirling around Earth. These tools send us weather images or map directions using electrical signals. Robotic space explorers like the Mars rovers also use battery power.

The Power Surge in Cities

Using electricity to travel changed human existence and the size of cities. Two hundred years ago, the most common ways to get around were by foot, horse, and steam engine. That is, until streetcars came along in the 1880s. These trains used electric motors. They drew power from cables strung above the street.

Cities swelled as streetcars became popular. People could live farther away from factories, smoke, and noise. Today, subways have taken the place of streetcars.

Going Up?

Electricity did not just make cities expand outward. It also raised them into the skies. The world's first skyscrapers sprang up thanks to electricity. Mighty electromagnets meant that construction cranes could lift heavy building materials ever higher. Electricity could also power elevators. Without these vertical "trains," people would have to climb hundreds or thousands of stairs to get home.

Electricity Working All Around Us

From toasters to defibrillators to super-fast trains to satellites, electricity has made our everyday lives easier. It has connected us across vast distances. It has helped us see more of the world around us and beyond our planet to other worlds in space. When electricity does the hard jobs, it moves more than electrons. In many ways, it helps move people too!

FACT

Around the world, nearly 760 million people live without regular use of electricity. Without electricity, people may not have access to clean, running water.

Jakarta, Indonesia, a modern city powered by electricity

GLOSSARY

atom (AT-uhm)—an element in its smallest form

circuit (SUHR-kuht)—a path for electricity to flow through

conductor (kuhn-DUHK-tuhr)—a material that lets electricity travel easily through it

electron (i-LEK-tron)—a negatively charged particle that whirls around the nucleus of an atom

insulator (IN-suh-late-ur)—a material that blocks an electrical current

neutron (NOO-trahn)—one of the very small parts in an atom's nucleus

proton (PRO-tahn)—one of the very small parts in an atom's nucleus; protons are positively charged

semiconductor (SEH-mee-kuhn-duhk-tuhr)—a material that electricity can only partly flow through

telegraph (TEL-uh-graf)—a machine that uses electronic signals to send messages over long distances

terminal (TUR-mih-nuhl)—a point through which electricity can enter or exit a battery

turbine generator (TUR-bine JEN-uh-ray-tur)—a machine that produces electricity as a fluid passes through curved blades attached to it

voltage (VOHL-tij)—the force of an electrical current

READ MORE

Amin, Anita Nahta. *Electricity*. Minneapolis: Jump!, Inc., 2022.

Eboch, M. M. *12 Biggest Breakthroughs in Energy Technology*. Mankato, MN: Top Rank, an imprint of Black Rabbit Books, 2025.

Midthun, Joseph. *Electricity*. Chicago: World Book, a Scott Fetzer Company, 2022.

INTERNET SITES

Electrical Safety for Kids: Educational Tips and Resources
mrelectric.com/blog/electrical-safety-for-kids-educational-tips-and-resources

Electricity for Kids
ducksters.com/science/electricity_101.php

Science of Electricity
eia.gov/kids/energy-sources/electricity/science-of-electricity.php

INDEX

atoms, 5, 15

batteries, 12, 13, 20, 21, 27

circuits, 12

conductors, 5, 21

cooling towers, 7, 8, 9

Edison, Thomas, 15

electrical currents, 8, 10, 14, 15, 19, 21

electromagnetism, 20–21, 26, 28

electrons, 4, 5, 8, 12, 14, 15, 28

generators, 6, 7, 8, 10

heat, 5, 14, 18, 19, 21, 23

insulators, 5

Internet, 4, 17

light, 4, 5, 6, 8, 13, 14, 15, 17, 18

machines, 5, 6, 19, 22, 23, 24, 25, 28

magnetism, 7, 8, 19, 20, 21, 25, 26

medical devices, 24, 25, 28

motors, 19, 20, 27

neutrons, 4, 5

power stations, 6, 9, 10

protons, 4, 5, 12

radio, 16

satellites, 27, 28

semiconductors, 14

substations, 10

transformers, 10, 11

transportation, 4, 22, 26, 27, 28

turbines, 6, 8, 9

Volta, Alessandro, 12

voltage, 5, 10, 11, 12, 13

wattage, 5

ABOUT THE AUTHOR

Jenny Mason is a story-hunter. She explores foreign countries, canyon mazes, and burial crypts to gather the facts that make the best true tales. She'll interview NASA engineers or sniff a 200-year-old skull. Her research knows no bounds! Jenny received her MFA in Writing for Children and Young Adults from the Vermont College of Fine Arts. She also holds a Master of Philosophy from Trinity College Dublin. Find all of Jenny's books and projects at jynnemason.com.